- THE -
LAKE DISTRICT
from the air

Photographs by

Simon Kirwan

Text by

Jerome Monahan

MYRIAD
LONDON

First published in 2006 by
Myriad Books Limited
35 Bishopsthorpe Road,
London SE26 4PA

Photographs copyright
© Simon Kirwan

Text copyright
© Jerome Monahan

ISBN 1 904 154 36 0

www.myriadbooks.com

Title page: Derwent
Water with Keswick
in the foreground;
right: Hopegill Head

CONTENTS

LAKE DISTRICT FROM THE AIR

FOR MOST PEOPLE the Lake District is experienced from the beautiful but busy honeypot destinations of Windermere, Ambleside, Grasmere and Keswick; few of us get the opportunity to explore this scenic corner of England from the vantage point of a Cessna 172 light aircraft, and to see the true splendour of Cumbria laid out in all its diverse glory. For *Lake District from the Air*, I was able to spend some glorious summer days high above the lakes, mountains and valleys of this most sublime part of the British Isles.

My first taste of the Lakeland fells came aged 12, when I stayed at Barrow House Youth Hostel, near Keswick at Borrowdale, on the banks of Derwent Water. Our school party made the ascent of Sca Fell Pike by the Corridor Route from Seathwaite, and so began my fascination with high places which has taken me to the hills and mountains not only of England, Ireland, Scotland and Wales but further afield, to the Alps of France and Italy, the High Tatras of Poland and Slovakia, the Usambara Mountains of Tanzania and the Nepal Himalaya.

Since that school trip all those years ago I have stood on the summit of Sca Fell Pike, and of all the other principal Lakeland peaks many times, in all weathers and in all seasons. This fascination with high places has been enhanced by producing the photography for this book, *The Lake District from the Air*. Cumbria is revealed anew, from the coastal towns to the west, with their islands and cliffs, to the castles and stone circles of the north, as well as the fells, lakes, rivers and mountains already so familiar from ground level.

Successful aerial photography depends on a combination of factors: the air must be clear, the sky preferably cloudless, and the sun bright. I am very fortunate to fly with John Seville, a highly experienced and very skilled aerial photographic pilot, who so far has resisted my attempts to persuade him to emulate the feat of 1926, when a light aircraft landed on the summit of Helvellyn. Nearby, Haweswater is the last nesting-place in England of the golden eagle. It has been my great privilege to fly over this marvellous landscape and see it from the perspective of these wonderful birds.

Simon Kirwan

SOUTHERN LAKE DISTRICT

The Southern Lake District is an area of fell, woodland and coastal expanse. It is dominated in the north by Grisedale Forest and defined in the south by the river Kent where it emerges into Morecambe Bay. It stretches up as far as the southern shore of Lake Windermere. It is an area rich in tourist opportunities boasting everything from fine walking to some of the best windsurfing in the UK in and around the islands south of Barrow-in-Furness. It is a far less rugged landscape than the rest of the Lakes and has a rich assortment of prosperous and unspoilt market towns to entice the visitor. These include Ulverston and Broughton-in-Furness, both prominent in their time as major trading centres.

SILVERDALE

Silverdale is a picturesque seaside village on the shores of Morecambe Bay. In season it is a popular holiday spot and boasts a wide variety of shops, cafes and pubs. An aerial view reveals the glorious natural hinterland beyond Silverdale – a hugely varied and tranquil landscape containing important limestone pavements and ancient woodland – home to myriad species of birds, insects and plants. It is has been designated an Area of Outstanding Natural Beauty and just one mile from the village is the Royal Society For the Protection of Birds' reserve at Leighton Moss. Morecambe Bay's spectacular stretches of coastal sand can be treacherous – and walking on the sands should only be undertaken with an experienced guide.

ARNSIDE

The village of Arnside appears to emerge from the thickly-wooded slopes of the Knott – a limestone headland looking over Morecambe Bay. The word "knott" means a rounded hill – one of many local terms thought to be derived from Viking settlers. It was once a busy port trading in slate, gunpowder, coal and pig-iron. The silting up of the Kent estuary, a process exacerbated by the building of the 50-arch railway viaduct across the sands in 1857, finally put paid to the town's marine significance. Today, Arnside is a bustling seaside resort and a popular retirement destination.

ARNSIDE TOWER

Condemned as a scourge, the *reivers* were cross-border raiders. Their winter-time attacks – carried out after the harvests were gathered and when they knew there would be rich pickings – survive today in both ballad and novel. Fear drove those that could afford it to build defensive pele towers within which they could hide and hope to sit out the reivers' depredations. One such pele survives at Arnside. The reivers' days were numbered when James I became joint monarch of Scotland and England in 1603, embarking on a concerted campaign to restore order to these lawless lands. Among the measures that proved highly successful was forbidding Border people to carry weapons and restricting their ownership of horses.

ROA ISLAND

To the south of Barrow-in-Furness at the north-west of Morecambe Bay, the landscape becomes an intricate mix of causeway-connected islands and inlets. One of the most prominent of these is Roa Island with its tiny village (population 100). Its largest house was built by the Furness industrialist HW Schneider and its seven cannons pointing out to sea are one of the island's most famous sights. In 1840 London banker John Abel Smith bought Roa Island as part of his plans to operate a train ferry from Piel Island to Fleetwood on the other side of the bay. Much of Roa Island's infrastructure, including its causeway and deep-water pier, were created as part of this venture. Today, Piel Island can be visited by ferry from Roa Island.

PIEL CASTLE

Moved by the sight of Piel Castle, in 1805 William Wordsworth wrote the following lines:

I was thy neighbour once, thou rugged Pile!
Four summer weeks I dwelt in sight of thee:
I saw thee every day! and all the while
Thy Form was sleeping on a glassy sea.

The castle was built in the 14th century by the abbots of Furness – a place of refuge and a means of policing seaborne trade with the Isle of Man. It may also have been a convenient way of keeping royal authorities at bay. The castle today is a ruin but its large central keep and outer defensive rings remain a prominent break on the horizon in this otherwise flat landscape.

PIEL ISLAND

Piel Island enjoys a rich history. Its first recorded name was Fotheray, derived from the Scandinavian terms for "fodder". In 1127 Piel was given to a local order of Savignac monks, who later merged with the Cistercian order. They developed Piel as a licensed port. On June 4 1487 Lambert Simnel landed at Piel claiming to be the Earl of Warwick (one of the Princes in the Tower) and rightful heir to the throne. He marched his mercenary army south towards Piel but was defeated at Stoke. Instead of being executed, Simnel was allowed to live out his days in King Henry VII's kitchens. The landlord of the Ship Inn on Piel is to this day nicknamed the King of Piel in commemoration of the rebellion.

FURNESS ABBEY

Furness Abbey was founded in 1123 and became in time the second richest Cistercian monastery in England after Fountains Abbey in Yorkshire. Though long ruined, the remaining structures hint strongly at the original grandeur of this remarkable site. Today it is still possible to get a good sense of the main precinct and outer court, the church itself and the chapter house plus the abbey's dormitory, infirmary and kitchen. The monks were responsible for boosting the local economy thanks to their wool and iron trading through nearby Walney Island – protected by the castle at Piel. The abbey's decline started during the terrible 14th century. Plague reduced the number of monks and much of the land it owned was leased out to tenant farmers. Its fate was sealed during the Reformation. Interest in the abbey grew during the Romantic period, the ruins proving a source of inspiration for both Wordsworth and the painter Turner. The abbey is now under the care of English Heritage.

BARROW-IN-FURNESS *(left and below)*

Barrow-in-Furness has a population of over 70,000 and is sited on the Furness Peninsula which protrudes into Morecambe Bay. It was once a world centre of steelmaking with significant shipyards but those industries are now in decline. Barrow is one of England's few planned towns and it retains its wide, tree-lined streets to this day. There are many fine churches and public buildings including the town hall, a legacy of James Ramsden, Barrow's most famous resident and the town's first mayor who conceived the idea of Barrow as a shipbuilding centre.

ULVERSTON

Ulverston won its official status as a market town in 1280, when Edward I granted it a royal charter – an event still celebrated each September at a special festival. It has produced a number of famous citizens, including George Fox, the founder of the Quaker movement and Stanley Jefferson, better known as Stan Laurel. Ulverston is home to the only Laurel and Hardy museum in the world. It was once a thriving inland port thanks to the construction of a canal in 1796 by engineer John Rennie. But the arrival of the railways put paid to that. Ulverston is now an attractive town well-known for its labyrinthine narrow cobbled streets. It is also a glass-making centre, producing the famous Heron and Cumbrian crystal. The town is traditionally the start of the 70-mile Cumbrian Way.

HOAD MONUMENT

The Hoad Monument is Ulverston's outstanding site – a landmark from which there are spectacular views of the Pennines and Morecambe Bay on clear days. It was built in 1850 in honour of the explorer and founder-member of the Royal Geographical Society, Sir John Barrow. The pepperpot-like structure is, in fact, a replica of the Eddystone Lighthouse found south-west of Plymouth. Captain Cook was one of Barrow's great admirers, having used many of his maps on his voyages. Barrow was also the definitive chronicler of the shipboard rebellion in 1789 that became famous as the Mutiny on the Bounty.

BROUGHTON-IN-FURNESS

Broughton-in-Furness came to prominence as a
strategic site on the river Duddon where it broadens
into an estuary. The name "Broughton" appropriately
derives from the word "stronghold". Its greatest
moment of economic importance was arguably in the
18th century when the town was a hub for local wool,
cattle and oak baskets. Each year the town celebrates
its market charter by having it read by the incumbent
mayor in the town square. The village was temporarily
home to Branwell Brontë who worked as a tutor at a
local school. The area is exceptionally lovely and
inspired Wordsworth to write:

> Majestic Duddon over smooth flat sands
> Gliding in silence with unfettered sweep!...

BROUGHTON TOWER

Yet more evidence of the Lakes' violent past –
Broughton Tower was originally a pele tower built in
1322 to defend the Broughton family from reiver raids.
Their fate was sealed, however, when they backed the
wrong side in Lambert Simnel's abortive attempt to
challenge the Tudor king Henry VII in 1487. It then
became the possession of the Stanleys – Earls of Derby
until they too backed the losing Royalist cause in the
English Civil War (1642-8). Since then the building has
been subject to continual extension and alteration.
It has also enjoyed numerous different changes in use
– from stronghold to family home and then a school.
It is now divided into private apartments.

BIRKER FELL (*right*)

The remote Birker fell with Devoke Tarn at its centre is a magnet for ramblers. A popular walk is to circumnavigate the tarn taking in the surrounding summits of Water Crag, Rough Crag, Seat How and White Pike. From here there are superb views north-east towards the high peaks of the western fells including Scafell and west towards the Ravenglass Estuary and the Irish Sea.

DEVOKE WATER (*below*)

Situated high on the isolated moorland of Birker Fell, Devoke Water is almost one mile (1.6km) long and is the largest tarn in the Lake District. On its north-west side the tarn is drained by Linbeck Gill (marked by a deep valley on the far side of the photograph) which cascades out of the tarn on its way to meet the river Esk in the valley below. The only sign of life in this desolate landscape is the deserted lodge/boathouse perched at the side of the water which can be seen in the foreground of the photograph.

NEWBY BRIDGE

Newby Bridge takes its name from the five-arched stone bridge
that spans the river Leven at the southernmost end of Windermere.
The photograph (left) is of the bridge and village as it appears looking
west while (above) the prospect north-east is perhaps even more
picturesque with the photograph taken high above the romantically-
named Great Wood. The substantial building to be seen in both
images is Newby Bridge Hotel, formally Newby Bridge Mansion. Built
in 1793 for the Machel family, it was one of the first great houses on

the banks of Windermere. William Wordsworth was a family friend
and today there is a poem by him to Lizzie, one of the Machel
children, on display in the hotel. In more recent times Arthur
Ransome, the author of *Swallows and Amazons*, stayed in the hotel.
Today, steam locomotives run from Haverthwaite through Newby
Bridge to Lakeside. Originally built in 1869 as a branch line of the
Furness railway, it connects with the Windermere steamers. The short
ride is a magnet for rail enthusiasts visiting the Lakes.

FELL FOOT

Hundreds of feet above High Parrock Wood, this view is taken looking due east towards Fell Foot Park and Gardens at the southern end of Windermere. Fell Foot was a typical late Victorian garden of rhododendrons, oaks and pines. The great house that once stood at the centre of these atmospheric grounds has long since been demolished, and after many years of neglect the National Trust is undertaking a programme to restore the garden and woods to their former glory. This attractive 18 acre (7ha) site is open throughout the year.

FINSTHWAITE

Just north of Newby Bridge lies the picturesque village of Finsthwaite. In the photograph (left) we see the village looking south-east with Lakeside in the distance and the unmistakeable bulge of land which narrows Windermere at its southernmost end. Finsthwaite Tower is situated near the village. It was built to honour the officers, seamen and marines of the Royal Navy who defeated the fleets of France, Spain and Holland in 1799.

CONISTON

The view below is taken high above Coniston Water looking back due west at the village of Coniston with Yowdale Beck in the middle distance. Coniston Water is famous as being the site of Donald Campbell's death in 1967 during his failed attempt in *Bluebird* to break the world water speed record.

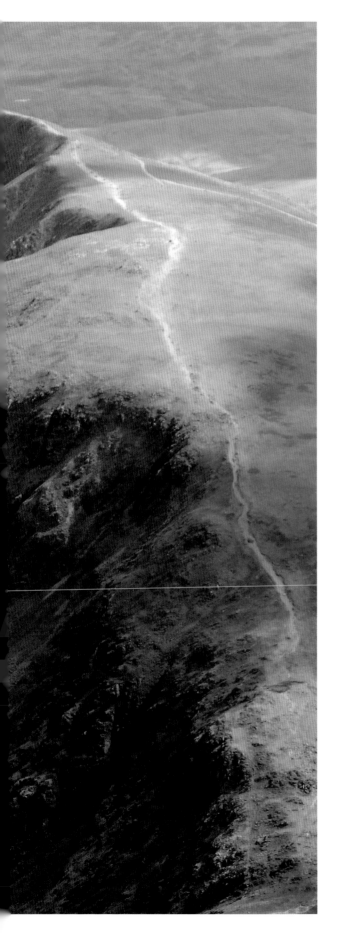

CONISTON OLD MAN

Almost identical views to the south-east (left and below) take in
Coniston Old Man, the second showing Low Water Tarn. In the distance
the shimmering expanse of water is Coniston, from which this peak derives part of its
name. The "Old Man" reaches the formidable height of 2,635ft (801m). Nearby is the peak
known as Wetherlam and between the two lies Levers Water.

LEVERS WATER

Its classification as a tarn suggests it should have a tear-drop shape, but as the photograph
suggests, it is far more diamond-like in appearance. One of the most popular of the routes
up to Coniston Old Man travels past Levers Water, along Levers Water Beck, through the
wonderfully named Boulder Valley and past the Pudding Stone. This vast rock never fails
in enticing walkers to make the effort to reach its mini-summit despite still having a fairly
long haul to the top of Coniston Old Man before them.

WESTERN LAKE DISTRICT

The Western region of the Lakes prides itself on its wide range of landscapes and myriad diversions. The coastline, which includes the Solway Firth and the Duddon Estuary, is particularly varied – a mix of sandy beaches and imposing sea cliffs, estuaries and sheltered coves. Its narrow coastal plain is home to many picturesque villages and hamlets, allowing the visitor access to the more rugged countryside to the east. Further inland are the spectacular valleys of Duddon, Eskdale and Wasdale. Elsewhere Borrowdale, Buttermere and Wasdale add to the challenges facing walkers and fell-climbers while sublime stretches of water, which include Buttermere, offer both the sailing and fishing enthusiast endless pleasures.

MUNCASTER CASTLE

A substantial and luxurious Lakeland country house that has grown up around a defensive pele tower, Muncaster Castle is built on land that was an important site even in Roman times. It has been home to the Pennington family since 1208 and has been through many transformations down the centuries – the most substantial of these occurring in 1862 when architect Anthony Salvin oversaw alterations and the rebuilding of the castle for the fourth Baron Muncaster. The castle is crammed with exquisite furniture and paintings including portraits by Joshua Reynolds and Gainsborough. One of its most famous items is the glass drinking bowl given to the family by Henry VI known as the "luck of Muncaster". The castle is said to be haunted by a mischievous jester. It is surrounded by a spectacular park and is home to an owl centre.

RIVER ESK

Eskdale and the river Esk that runs through it have been described as a "hidden gem". The river rises in the fells at Esk Hause, passes through the Great Moss and enters the valley proper via a series of waterfalls. On its more lowland course, the Esk waters some of the most stunning oak woodland in Cumbria. Within the valley are numerous delightful villages including Boot, Eskdale Green and Ravenglass – the latest manifestations of over 4,000 years of human settlement in the region. It was here that the Roman emperor Agricola built four forts, though the Esk valley owes more to its later Norse settlers who recognised enough of their native Scandinavia in this valley to make it their permanent home. Today the Esk valley is a walkers' paradise.

ST BEES HEAD

St Bees Head is the westernmost part of the Lake District. It is a site of beauty for walkers – its four-mile clifftop path being the first on the route of the 190-mile (305km) Coast-to-Coast walk. This is a dangerous area for shipping as proven by the lighthouse, which dates from 1886-7, the latest in a series of warning beacons; the rusting hulks of long-forgotten ships can be seen on the shingle at the foot of the 300-foot cliffs. These are a haven for many species of seabird including kittiwakes, herring gulls, razorbills, puffins, ravens, stonechats and red-legged guillemots. Today the site is a bird sanctuary. Legend has it that St Bega – the daughter of an Irish king – was miraculously brought here by an angel. She went on to found a nunnery. The only surviving sign of the local religious order survives in the red sandstone porch of the parish church surmounted by a lovely carving of St George and the dragon.

EGREMONT

Egremont owes its original fortunes to dyeing and weaving. The local iron ore deposits are famous for the red hue that would stain those that mined it, earning them the nickname "the red men of Cumbria". Egremont is a traditional market town at the foot of Uldale Valley and Dent Fell. It is home to the Florence mine, the last deep iron ore mine in western Europe. One of its most famous sights is the castle. Wordsworth celebrates the legend of the *Horn of Egremont* in one of his poems. It could only be blown by the rightful heir and this foiled the dastardly plans of Hubert de Lucy who attempted to usurp his older brother's title and wife by claiming he had died while on the Crusades. At the crucial moment the horn is said to have sounded spontaneously signalling that Hubert's plot to have his older brother murdered out in the Holy Lands had failed.

WHITEHAVEN

Originally a harbour for the monks at nearby St Bees, Whitehaven really took off in the 17th century thanks to its location near substantial local coal and iron ore reserves. In the 1750s it was England's third most important port but its shallow waters ultimately meant it could not compete with Liverpool. The decline froze the town, preserving its Georgian houses, and today there are over 250 listed buildings. The white round building to the right of the harbour is The Beacon – now a museum celebrating the town's maritime past.

SCAFELL

Scafell at 3,162ft (964m) and Scafell Pike at 3,210ft (977m) are two of England's five highest peaks. They both command celebrated views across the landscape of the Lake District National Park. They are part of the Cumbrian Mountains formed as volcanoes when the North American and Eurasian continents collided. Together with Ben Nevis and Mount Snowdon, Scafell Pike is one of the three summits to be conquered in just 24 hours in order to meet the conditions of the Three Peaks Challenge. The ascent offers stunning views over Wast Water to the west and the Langdale Pikes to the east. Scafell is a challenging climb, the rapidly changing weather posing an additional hazard to the unwary. It is separated from Scafell by a ridge called Mickledore. Its summit is marked by a huge cairn.

SCAFELL *(above)* AND SCAFELL PIKE *(right)*

It is thought the first recorded non-Lakelander to climb Scafell was the poet Coleridge. He took with him an ink horn and paper and, having reached the summit, set about recording his feelings to Sarah Hutchinson in a letter dated August 5 1802. He made a helter-skelter descent, ignoring straightforward ways, preferring to take a precipitate direct route down claiming that he was too indolent to bother with looking for other paths. He wrote: *"I ascended Sca'Fell by the side of a torrent, and climbed & rested, rested & climbed, till I gained the very summit of Sca'Fell – believed by the Shepherds here to be higher than even Helvellyn or Skiddaw... O my God! What enormous Mountains these are close by me..."*

WASDALE

This is one of the most desolate and wild of the Lake District valleys. It is famous for Scafell Pike, Wast Water, the region's deepest lake and St Olaf's, the smallest church. The valley is fringed with spectacular scree slopes – particularly at Wast Water where they plunge over 2,000ft (610m). Near the lake is the tiny settlement of Wasdale Head with its church said to have roof beams that once served as the timbers of a Viking longboat. Every November Wasdale celebrates the World's Biggest Liar competition.

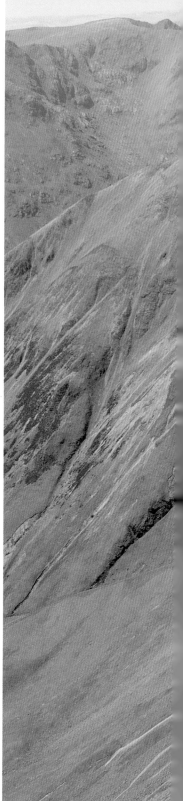

GREAT GABLE

Great Gable is a beautifully proportioned mountain – so much so that it is used as the centrepiece motif
for the Lake District National Park logo. On its slopes can be seen the remains of past industrial times including
slateworks and the line of a former tramway. One track named Moses Trod is thought to have been a favourite route
for smugglers and their contraband liquor. On clear days climbers and walkers are rewarded with splendid views of
Wasdale and the sights at the summit are even more special – the panorama including every peak in Lakeland.

PILLAR AND PILLAR ROCK

The Pillar Rock is a 500ft (152m) outcrop halfway up to the summit of the Pillar Mountain – which at 2,926 feet (892m) is the eleventh highest summit in the Lakes. The Rock has long been beloved of mountaineers, offering a variety of routes of varying difficulty. It was here in 1913 that the young George Mallory gained early experience ahead of his several attempts on Everest during the inter-war years. One of the climbs is still known as the Mallory route. The mountain itself is considered one of the easier of the big Lakeland peaks to climb – the effort rewarded with awesome views, particularly (as shown in the image right) the 2,000 foot drop into the Ennerdale Valley.

HIGH CRAG

The High Stile range of peaks photographed from just below low cloud casts a
brooding presence over Buttermere and the small settlement of the same name.
The range is made up of High Crag, High Stile, the Hay Stacks and Red Pike and is
one of the most popular of the harder walking routes in the Lakes. To begin with the
route is through woods and waterfalls but this quickly gives way to open treeless
countryside as you near the summit. Even in these upper reaches there is increasing
evidence of heavy erosion of some paths due to the high numbers of walkers visiting
the area. The photograph above looks south-east away from Buttermere Fell and the
one below shows the spectacular drop to Buttermere from High Crag taking in the
outcrop known as the Grey Crags.

BUTTERMERE

Many claim that Buttermere is one of the Lake District's most beautiful locations. Without the unique geology of the valley of the river Cocker, it would probably have boasted a single expanse of water, but progressive silting has resulted in the emergence of three smaller lakes, of which Buttermere is one. This stretch of water is about a mile long and approximately 1,500 feet across and is encompassed by mountains. It is home to a number of extremely rare species of fish such as the Arctic charr. The photograph above shows the view north towards Buttermere Moss and the Goat Cragg; and, right, the sight from above Scale Beck looking south-east towards Buttermere village and the fertile pasture separating Crummock Water from Buttermere.

CRUMMOCK WATER

This view above Melbreak looks east towards Grasmoor and Whiteless Pike across Crummock Water. Beneath this vantage point is Scale Force, the Lake District's highest waterfall and one of many mountain rivers that feed the lake. Crummock Water is owned by the National Trust who apply a rigid ban on watersports although those that carry their boats to the lake by hand are allowed to sail or row there. In such a place it is not hard to imagine why the painter John Constable felt the Lake District contained "the finest scenery that ever was".

BUTTERMERE

The Lake District tourist industry has its roots in the search among the well-to-do in the late 18th century for the sublime in nature. Of course tranquillity and innocence, the factors that drew people here, are the first casualties when a place and its people become the focus of intrusive curiosity and admiration. Mary Palmer, daughter of the inkeepeer at the Fish Hotel, was an early victim – celebrated for her beauty and simplicity by Wordsworth, nicknamed The Maid of Buttermere, but eventually tricked into a bigamous marriage by a rogue named John Hatfield. He was hanged, but not before news of the scandal had reached a wide public thanks to the Keswick correspondent of the London newspapers – Samuel Taylor Coleridge.

In the views above and right, Buttermere appears serene and peaceful, with little evidence of the "madding crowd". The view south-east down the valley towards Fleetwith Pike is as breathtaking as ever.

GRASMOOR

At 2,795ft (852m) Grasmoor is an imposing presence next to Crummock Water – its sharp cut ridges or arêtes and steep precipices a tribute to the glaciers that carved its shape from tough igneous rock during the last Ice Age. It is the highest of the north-western lake fells. Grasmoor is a favourite challenge for hardier visitors to the Lakes who are rewarded on reaching the summit by a series of ridge-walk circuits taking in wonderful views in all directions. The word "gras" has nothing to do with "grass" but derives from *grice* meaning "wild boar". The silver stream (below) is Gasgale Gill as it makes its way down from Cauledale Hause. It passes the imposing Gasgale Crags as it cuts a direct course down to Crummock Water.

FLEETWITH PIKE

Stand at the head of Buttermere and look south to where the road snakes its way up to the Honister Pass and Fleetwith Pike is an unmistakeable imposing presence. Reaching 2,126ft (648m), it is the mass of rock on its flank – the Honister Crags – that make it so memorable. Walkers have long braved this tough ascent in order to reach the high ground and so enjoy the view north-west back up the valley. The mountain offers superb panoramas down the Buttermere, Crummock, and Loweswater valleys. Having reached the summit, the walker can then quickly gain access to the higher plateau for more leisurely exploration.

HAYSTACKS

At 1,910 feet (582m) Haystacks offers some fine views of Buttermere, Crummock Water and Ennerdale Water. It is a fairly modest peak compared to some of its neighbours, but it stands in an important position at the head of the Buttermere valley. To the south are the towering crags of the Pillar range whilst to the north is the somewhat less imposing Newlands range. Right beside it are Great Gable and High Stile. It was the proximity of Haystacks to such spectacular ranges and overlooking such vistas that made it a favourite spot for Alfred Wainwright – the man who did so much to popularise walking and exploring the Lake District in the 20th century.

KNOTT RIGG

We are looking down on Newlands Valley towards the north-east. The head of the valley is here dominated by Knott Rig which climbs to over 1,804ft (550m), and on the opposite side are Robinson Crags which are even steeper and reach a further 200 metres into the sky. Walkers approach the Rigg from this direction and take the route up from Newlands Hause – just to the bottom of the picture. The Keskadale Beck follows the valley bottom heading off to join Newlands Beck in the valley proper just around the next bend.

NEWLANDS VALLEY

Newlands is a beautiful and comparatively quiet valley. It is not heavily populated and has not been touched by the commercialism of many other Lakeland valleys. Its farms do a brisk trade in bed and breakfast accommodation and offer an alternative experience to more hectic Keswick. One of the most delightful paths runs alongside the valley's beck or stream. The imposing crags in shadow are Red Knott where old workings are testament to the leadmining operations that used to be conducted here. Even more startling is the view north up the valley towards Skiddaw.

CENTRAL LAKE DISTRICT

The heart of the Lake District is a rocky one. It is a place of wide contrasts too. As well as its mountains it is home to many picturesque villages rich in history and culture. Its scenery is among the most beautiful in the world and it has always been a place of wonder and inspiration to poets, artists and the general public who have long regarded this as a place of solace and recreation. It was here that Beatrix Potter made her permanent home and also where the Romantic poets and writers of the early 19th century gathered – drawn to the area by its beauty and the presence of William Wordsworth and his family in Grasmere and in his home at Rydal Mount. It is a land beloved of anglers and mountaineers too with the lakes and fells providing both with endless challenges.

BOWNESS-ON-WINDERMERE

Bowness-on-Windermere covers about 12 miles (19km) of the western shore of Lake Windermere. It is a thriving, bustling town. The view east from the town over the lake is delightful. It includes Belle Isle and the heavily wooded Claife Heights rising to Latterbarrow at 803ft (245m). Bowness owes its greatest period of expansion to the arrival of the railway line from Oxenholme and Kendal in 1847. The town's Victorian roots are unmistakeable thanks to the many late 19th-century residences overlooking the lake built by wealthy Lancashire businessmen. They are now mostly hotels. The old Bowness is preserved to the rear of St Martin's church where there is a labyrinth of narrow streets collectively known as Lowside. When William Wordsworth in *The Prelude* describes bounding *"the hill shouting amain/ A lusty summons to the further shore/For the old Ferryman"* – he is referring to the Bowness ferry that he frequently took across Windermere.

BELLE ISLE

One-mile long, Belle Isle is a wooded island in the middle of Windermere. It was landscaped in the 18th and 19th centuries but it has a known history dating back to Roman times when Ambleside's governor chose its secure situation for the location of a villa. It was once known as the Great Island – home to a family called Philipson and then a Mr English who instructed the architect John Plaw to build the elegant portico-fronted house that stands there today. Following its sale for £1,720 to mining entrepreneur John Curwen in 1774, it was renamed Belle after his wife Isabella. Their descendants lived here until 1993. The house is still in private hands.

WINDERMERE

William Wordsworth loved Windermere and frequently rowed on it. He was a fervent critic of increased tourism to the area in the latter part of his life and wrote letters of protest to the authorities when a railway link was proposed for the area. But his objections were not to everyone's taste and met with the following response from the Board of Trade in 1845:

"We must therefore state that an argument which goes to deprive the artisan of the offered means of occasionally changing his narrow abode, his crowded streets, his wearisome task and unwholesome toil, for the fresh air, and the healthful holiday which sends him back to his work refreshed and invigorated – simply that individuals who object on the grounds above stated may retain to themselves the exclusive enjoyment of scenes which should be open alike to all, provided the enjoyment of them shall not involve the infringement of private rights, appears to us to be an argument wholly untenable..."

WINDERMERE

Windermere is 10.5 miles long and is England's longest lake. It takes its name from a Viking chieftan called Vinandr – Vinandr's Mere became Windermere. The lake is formed from the gouging effect of glaciers that once moved down the valley 10,000 years ago. Today, Windermere is fed by many rivers including the Rothay and the Brathay and the southern outflow is the Leven.

The lake is well-stocked with fish including pike, perch, salmon and trout and a rare fish called the "charr" – hugely popular in 18th-century London. In the 19th century William Wordsworth would gaze across the Lake and later write: *"I overlooked the bed of Windermere,/...A universe of Nature's fairest forms..."*

THE TEAL

The *Teal*, built in 1936, is one of three steamers operated by Windermere Lake Cruises Ltd providing pleasure trips on the water. The other two are the *Tern*, built in 1891 and the *Swan* constructed in 1938. Steamers have been a feature of life on the lake since 1845 when the Windermere Steam Yacht Company was formed. There has also been a

ferry on the lake for over 500 years which crosses at the narrowest part at Ferry Nab to the south of Bowness. It was once a flat-bottomed wooden boat with long oars. During a fearsome storm in 1635 the ferry capsized and 47 people and 11 horses returning from a wedding in Hawkshead were drowned.

VIEWS ACROSS AMBLESIDE

The market town of Ambleside is situated at the northern end of Windermere. It has a long history encompassing Roman and Viking settlement. From the middle ages, its fortunes were wedded to wool-making enhanced, as industrial processes advanced, by the might of nearby Stock Ghyll Force – a 60ft (18m) high waterfall capable of driving a number of watermills. By the late 18th century wool manufacture was in decline but the 1800s saw the start of a tourist industry that again brought prosperity and continues undiminished to the present day.

The vista north from above Windermere over Ambleside (below) shows the land beyond climbing to Scandale Fell – the source of Scandale Beck that skirts the upper reaches of the town.

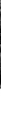

AMBLESIDE

Today Ambleside boasts a wide variety of attractions including the Armitt Museum with its special focus on Beatrix Potter and her animal stories. The Church of St Mary the Virgin has a chapel dedicated to William Wordsworth. The church is one of a very few places that still carry out an annual "rush-bearing" ceremony – involving the blessing of reeds destined to provide a kind of crude carpet for the cold earth or stone flags of the church floor. The photograph below shows the scene to the south-west from above Wansfell showing Ambleside and the tranquil view out across Windermere.

LAKESIDE

The view over Lakeside (left) looking south-west reveals the vast Finsthwaite plantation – the tracks of the Lakeside and Haversthwaite Railway clearly visible snaking along the valley beside the Haversthwaite river. Lakeside is a key tourist centre – a hub for sailing enthusiasts and day visitors drawn to the Aquarium of the Lakes with its displays providing insights into the area's unique underwater eco-systems. The steam railway is also a major draw giving passengers a taste of the golden age of rail travel over its three and a half mile track to Haversthwaite.

LOUGHRIGG FELL

Hovering over Loughrigg Fell, the photograph captures a view across Loughrigg Tarn looking due south towards the settlement of Skelwith Bridge. The photograph on the right catches the vista to the north looking across the Fell towards Grasmere with the pass between The Great Tongue and Grasmere Common plainly visible. Loughrigg Fell is a prominent 1,099ft (335m) hill standing at the end of a long ridge dropping down from High Raise. It is a favourite walkers' destination with the preferred route leading to Loughrigg Terrace with views of Grasmere, Helm Crag and the Fairfield group of mountains. Loughrigg Fell is one of the most popular hills in the lakes, with over 100 paths to the top. Another attraction on Loughrigg Terrace are some quite remarkable caves caused by quarrying.

RYDAL WATER

The view is due west over Rydal Water with Grasmere in the distance and the heights of Silver How and Lang How on the horizon. Rydal Water is just three-quarters of a mile long but it is a place rich in beauty and important associations. It was one of Wordsworth's best-loved spots and there is a view dedicated to him to this day. Rydal is a tiny village but its houses include Rydal Mount. The Wordsworth family moved there in 1813 and rented the house continuously for 46 years, until the death of Mary in 1859.

WRAY CASTLE

Wray Castle is a 19th-century confection. Built in 1840 in the Gothic Revival-style, it was home to a Dr Dawson, a retired Liverpool surgeon. When she was just 16, Beatrix Potter's family rented the castle during a visit to the Lakes in 1882. The experience of staying at Wray and seeing the Lakes had a profound effect on her, influencing her later decision to make her home nearby and to buy most of the land around the castle with the royalties from her books. The castle was given to the National Trust in 1929.

GHYLL HEAD RESERVOIR

The view south-east takes in Ghyll Head Reservoir – a short distance from Newby Bridge at the southern end of Windermere. This man-made lake, which is one of the foremost fishing spots in Lakeland, is described in *Carlson's Fishing Tackles* as a "lovely 11-acre water with deep areas nearest the road and shallows at the far end". Anglers are alerted to "lots of buzzers, damsels, small rudd fry, olives, sedges and bracken clock beetles", as well as "larger creatures including badgers and red deer in the early morning". The mysterious language of the angler is almost like poetry to the uninitiated: "fishes best on floating line and imitative patterns but a sinker and a hot orange lure can always be relied on to save the day. This water is very much on or off..."

ESTHWAITE WATER

The bird's-eye view above Hawkshead Hall Park is spectacular looking south-east over Esthwaite Water. The village of Near Sawrey in the distance nestles on the far bank. It is the site of Hill Top, the home of Beatrix Potter. Esthwaite Water is one of the least visited of the 16 major lakes in the region. It is small and shallow but it teems with fish and wildlife. In the summer, water lilies make it an even more lovely sight. A footpath meanders around the lake from the north-western corner offering the walker wonderful views on the one side of Grisedale Forest Park and the Claife Heights on the other. Among keen fishermen Esthwaite Water is known for its excellent trout fishing and top notch pike and coarse fishing.

THE LANGDALE PIKES

The Pike of Stickle, pictured above, also known as Pike O' Stickle, reaches a height of 2,326ft (709m) and can be found in the valley of Great Langdale. The Pike of Stickle rises steeply from Langdale, culminating in a pyramidal summit from which there are awesome views of the head of the valley, the fells of Bow Fell and Crinkle Crags. Pike of Stickle is famous as the site of a neolithic stone axe factory to be found on the scree slope on the southern slope of the fell. It was one of the most important such prehistoric factories in Europe. Early man was attracted to this spot by the vein of greenstone, a highly durable igneous rock, which surfaces here. The Langdale Pikes include Harrison Stickle and Pavey Ark, pictured below and right with Stickle Tarn.

GRASMERE

Grasmere was described by Wordsworth as "the loveliest spot that man has found" and is a short stroll from the village of the same name. Grasmere lies in the heart of the Lake District, centrally placed between Ambleside, Keswick and Coniston. It is probably the most visited village in the Lake District, because of its associations with the Wordsworths – William, his wife Mary and sister Dorothy – who made Dove Cottage their home from 1799 until 1808. Another focal point is the Church of St Oswald where William and his family lie

GRASMERE VIEWS

In the photograph left, high above Dow Bank, the vista takes in the lake and Grasmere village; beyond, the Rothay valley with Buttermere in the foreground. Above is the south-east prospect across Grasmere and, below, Grasmere village photographed from above Lord Crag on the slopes leading to Rydal Fell.

buried. In early August one of the few remaining rush-bearing ceremonies in the lakes takes place here. Later in the month the Grasmere Sports are held with displays of wrestling, fell racing and hound trailing.

DERWENT WATER

Fed by the river Derwent, Derwent Water lies to the south of Keswick. It contains several islands – three of which are to be seen in the photograph, left. These are Derwent Isle, Lords Island and tiny Rampsholme Island just in view. The steep drop of Lady's Rake Crag is clearly visible in the distance. Friars Crag is the promontory jutting into the lake just beyond Derwent Isle. Friars Crag achieved its name because it was believed to be the embarkation point for monks making a pilgrimage to St Herbert's Island, located in the centre of Derwent Water. It is thanks to Canon Rawnsley, vicar of nearby Crosthwaite Church on the edge of Keswick, that much of this land has been so remarkably preserved. He was a founder of the National Trust. On his death in 1920 Friars Crag was one of several sites given to the Trust as his memorial. The view above, north-east over Keswick, shows Lonscale Fell towering 2,345ft (715m) above the valley.

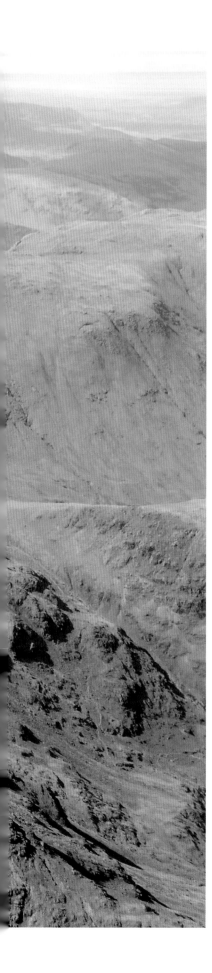

BOWFELL

The view north-west over Bowfell is one of the most spectacular in the Lakes looking out onto Great End and the Great Gable heights. It lies to the east of Scafell. Among its attractions are the Great Slab and the drop down over the crag at Bowfell Links. It is an impressive mountain, flanked to the south by Crinkle Crags and to the north by the Langdale Pikes. The Band is the favoured route up Bowfell. The panoramic views from the summit are breathtaking with the Pennines to the east and, on clear days, the sight of the Isle of Man to the west.

GLARAMARA

At the heart of one of the mountainous parts of the Lakes, Glaramara lies to the north of Langdale Fell and to the immediate west of Stonethwaite Fell. The ridge is considered to be a branch of the Scafell massif.

Glaramara is mentioned in Sir Walter Scott's poem *The Bride of Triermain*, which describes how King Arthur...

> *...journeyed like errant knight the while,*
> *And sweetly the summer sun did shine,*
> *On mountain, moss and moor.*
> *Above his solitary track*
> *Rose Glaramara's ridgy back...*

ELTERWATER

Elterwater lies in an attractive setting, a few miles west of Ambleside, hidden behind Loughrigg and Silver How, at the entrance to Great Langdale. Here we see it from the south-east looking north-west, with the village of Elterwater just in view. Langdale Beck flows through the village down to Elterwater. This stretch of water is sometimes known as the "Lake of the Swans" and is dominated by the twin peaks of Harrison Stickle and Pike of Stickle, which rise above the hills of bracken and mixed woodland.

EASEDALE TARN

Here we see the view west taking in Easedale Tarn with its crags climbing 900 feet to create a natural amphitheatre. The valley is littered with boulders rounded by the force of ice scraping over them. Sour Milk Gill, so called because of its white churning water, exits from the tarn. To reach Easedale Tarn a two-mile walk is required from Grasmere. According to the poet Thomas de Quincey, Easedale Tarn was "a chapel within a cathedral" and "the most gloomily sublime" of all the tarns he knew.

EASTERN LAKE DISTRICT

The eastern part of the Lake District is dominated by a great north to south ridge – the Helvellyn Range. This runs from Clough Head with its grassy slopes to Seat Sandal. Helvellyn has been described as "a wall of ten miles of 2,500 feet plus summits with grassy western slopes, but impressive rocky corries and crags on the eastern side". One of the most famous of the peaks is collectively known as the Fairfield group and this is found at the south of the range. It too follows the same pattern of slope and crag with towering rock faces and hidden valleys spilling into the Patterdale valley. The Fairfield group culminates in the harsh landscape overlooking the Kirkstone Pass – the highest road in the Lakes and a bleak spot famous for its apparitions. The far eastern fells lie on the other side of Patterdale. High Street is one of its most famous landmarks and at 2,717ft (828m) is the highest point on the ridge. It boasts spectacular crags dropping to the hidden valleys of Mardale and Haweswater. To the south are the fells overlooking Kentmere.

HAWESWATER RESERVOIR

The north and south ends of the serpentine Haweswater Reservoir (above and right) fill the valley between Bampton Common in the west and Swindale Common to the east. When the valley was flooded in 1935 to create a water supply for Manchester, the main casualty were the picturesque villages of Mardale Green and Measand, both of which were demolished. Among the most significant losses was the ancient Dun Bull Hotel at Mardale Green. The village church was dismantled and the stone used to construct the dam, and all the bodies in the churchyard were exhumed and re-buried at Shap. During periods of drought the remains of the village's buildings are revealed and invariably hit the headlines.

HAWESWATER & HAYESWATER

The southernmost end of the Haweswater Dam showing the wooded spur of land called The Rigg and the High Street ridge beyond is seen in the photograph above, as it culminates in Mardale Waters and Harter Fell. It was considered an engineering feat as it was the first hollow buttress dam in the world, having being constructed using 44 separate buttressed units joined by flexible joints. There is a 4.5ft (1.4m) wide parapet running the length of the dam and, from this, extra water supplies can be seen entering the reservoir from the adjoining valleys of Heltondale and Swindale – brought there by

tunnels. Commenting on the Haweswater Dam in his *Pictorial Guide to the Far Eastern Lakeland Fells*, Alfred Wainwright said: "...*man works with such clumsy hands, gone forever are the quiet wooded bays and shingly shores that nature had fashioned so sweetly in the Haweswater of old: how aggressively ugly is the tidemark of the new Haweswater*".

Hayeswater Reservoir (right) lies a few miles to the west, near Hartsop. The photograph shows the distinctive curved ridge of High Street, named after the Roman road that ran over its summit, linking the forts of Brocavum near Penrith and Galava at Ambleside.

SHAP ABBEY

The remains of Shap Abbey reveal the withdrawn life the original monks sought when they decided to settle here in the late 12th century. They belonged to an order that dressed in white and valued solitude and simplicity. As the centuries passed so did the wealth and opulence of the abbey. The most ostentatious proof of their increasing worldliness is the huge bell tower constructed in about 1500. Shap was the last abbey to be dissolved during the Reformation by Henry VIII. Its last service was in 1540. Stone from the abbey was used to build nearby Shap town's market hall, and much of the carved stonework was removed for use in Lowther Castle.

WET SLEDDALE RESERVOIR

Wet Sleddale Reservoir seen from the north-east with the heather-covered open land of Shap Fells spreading out into the distance. Along with the Haweswater Reservoir, it was constructed to supply Manchester with a supply of fresh water. The valley in which it is located once belonged to Shap Abbey. The reservoir's name is appropriate due to the amount of rainfall in the area. Its main claim to fame in modern times is Sleddale Hall, just out of image at the far end of the reservoir. This has become a place of pilgrimage for fans of the 1987 cult movie *Withnail and I*. The hall was the location of Crow Cragg – the site in the film of perhaps the most appalling weekend break ever conceived.

KENDAL AND KENDAL CASTLE

Kendal's limestone buildings have earned it the nickname "The Auld Grey one" and its location has consolidated it as the "Gateway to the Lakes". Kendal is often overlooked by visitors eager to press on to the Lake District proper, but to do so is to miss out on the charms of this underestimated town. Among its treasures is Holy Trinity Church – Cumbria's largest parish church. The local museum is also a must-see with a permanent exhibition dedicated to Alfred Wainwright whose sketches and descriptions of his favourite walks have popularised visiting and walking in Cumbria and beyond. The photograph (left) shows the view north across the town with the river Kent in view.

Kendal Castle commands high ground to the west of the town. The surviving remains are of a 12th-century structure and they include two towers and connecting stone ramparts. Its presence is a reminder of Kendal's violent past – frequently the object of Scots invasions. Richard II granted the castle to the Parr family, but it is thought unlikely that Katherine Parr, Kendal's most famous daughter, was actually born there. Today, the landscaped slopes beneath the ruins are a favourite walking and picnicking spot.

LEVENS

The village of Levens lies at the head of the estuary of the same name, which leads down to Morecambe Bay. The photograph (above) is taken immediately above the A6 and A590. The imposing St John the Evangelist church (built in 1828) is plainly in view at the bottom of the picture. Levens overlooks the Lyth Valley and was listed as *Lefuenes* in the Domesday Book. This sheltered valley is renowned for damson production and visitors flock to the area when the trees are in full blossom.

SIZERGH CASTLE

Sizergh Castle's south-east facing elevation (below) shows its ornamental pond and gardens. Like so many of Cumbria's castles, Sizergh was originally a pele tower built in the 14th century. It was home to the Strickland family for more than 750 years – passing to them by marriage when an heiress of the Deincourt family married into their ranks bringing the castle first given her family by Henry II in the 1170s. The tower acquired a great hall in 1450, and further additions were made to make the house more habitable in Tudor times. It has a ghost – that of a medieval woman starved to death by her husband. Her screams are still said to echo around the corridors. In addition to the castle there are 14 acres of gardens which were first laid out in the 18th century.

RED TARN

Red Tarn (above), high above Patterdale Common, is so-named because it resembles the colour of mercury when observed from the east. It is often cited as the perfect example of a corrie – the birthplace of a glacier. In a former Ice Age a "niche glacier" would form once an accumulation of snow reached a certain size and underlying pressure. The increased erosion both above and below ground ("nivation") would eventually create amphitheatre-type hollows with a characteristic rock "lip". It is this shape that means a corrie accumulates water in times when the glaciers retreat. Today Red Tarn is home to the rare schelly – one of three protected species of freshwater fish in the Lakes.

HELVELLYN

Helvellyn, at 3,118ft (950m), is one of only four peaks in the Lake District that climb above 3,000ft (915m). It is a must for any climber or serious walker visiting the area. Striding Edge is one of the most spectacular sights in the Lakes: an arête created by glacial action. Helvellyn's flat summit meant it was chosen by John Leeming and Bert Hinkler in 1926 for the first successful British mountain-top landing and take-off by plane.

The photograph (far right) looks north-west along Striding Edge with Lower Man at Helvellyn's summit; Thirlmere Water is in the distance. On the left, Striding Edge drops sharply to the westernmost end of Red Tarn.

STRIDING EDGE

A spectacular view of Striding Edge (left) photographed from above the Hole-in-the-Wall – looking due west. It is no wonder that this bizarre and spectacular landscape attracts tourists in large numbers. But what is worrying is that so many set out unprepared for the journey. Among experienced hill and mountain climbers in the Lake District the sight of poorly-clad and inappropriately-shod day-trippers attempting to reach Helvellyn along Striding Edge is a major source of annoyance. For such people a sudden change in the weather or their own lack of fitness – or the dramatic drops from The Edge itself – can make the experience a terrifying one.

THIRLMERE

Here we see the view north along Thirlmere – in the distance the wooded slopes to the west that form the foothills of High Seat. To the east Great How, also heavily wooded with spruce and larch, emerges from the valley flats. The original Thirlmere was a smaller lake than it is today, but the need for water in Manchester necessitated the building of a dam at the valley's north end between 1890 and 1894 and flooding of the valley bottom. Thirlmere, once an isolated place, has now been opened up by the presence of a minor road, plainly in view in the photograph on the western side. An effort is also being made to transform the woodland to create a more mixed habitat.

FAIRFIELD

Fairfield sits at the head of the valley immediately north of Ambleside. The Fairfield Horseshoe is one of the best known of the Lake District round-route walks during which it is possible to see wonderful panoramas across Rydale – particularly at Fairfield's summit. From there most of the Lake District peaks are visible and it is an ideal spot for viewing Helvellyn. For an adrenalin rush it is also recommended to peer over Fairfield's edge to inspect the complex corrie network at the head of Deepdale. The photograph on the left shows the view over the top of the Fairfield Horsehoe into Fairfield Tarn looking west. The photograph (above) illustrates the spectacle along the Horseshoe, taking in the gentler ascent to the peak up the Great Tongue from Town Head.

FAIRFIELD

Here the high-altitude photography gives three splendid views of the Fairfield Horseshoe showing the Rydal Head cliffs as they drop from a height of over 800 metres. The standard route up takes in the eastern ridge crossing Low Pike, High Pike, Dove Crag and Hart Crag and the return trip down is along the western ridge over Great Rigg, Heron Pike and Nab Scar – from which there are further fine views of Rydal and Grasmere. The last leg involves a return to Ambleside via Rydal Hall. The journey takes the walker through a dizzying series of landscapes including fellside lanes, woodland, steep ridges, high mountain ridges and, of course, Fairfield's stony summit plateau.

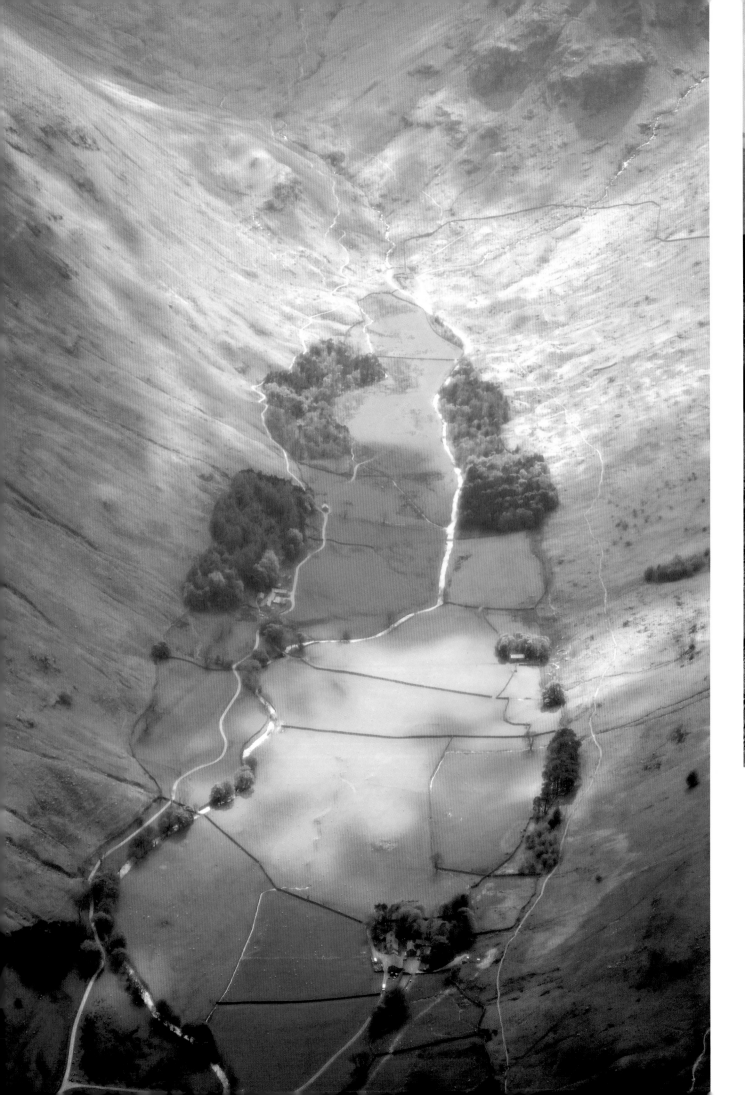

GRISEDALE

Like a lozenge of emerald green, the valley bottom of Grisedale lies wedged between the steeply rising ground mounting to Patterdale to the north and Deepdale to the south. The view (left) is the one to the south-east down Grisedale Valley. At the head of the valley the gradient climbs sharply to St Sunday and Eagle Crags. In old Norse, "Grisedale" means the "valley where young pigs were kept".

KIRKSTONE PASS

The photograph above shows the vista due north looking up the Kirkstone Pass towards Brothers Water, the high ground of Patterdale in sight and Ullswater just revealed in the far distance. At 1,489ft (454m) it is the highest road pass in the Lakes. This is not a road for a novice driver and yet in the summer it is filled with caravans and cars. Here is Thomas de Quincey writing about it in *Excursion over Kirkstone Pass in 1807*: "In some parts it is almost frightfully steep; for the road being only the original mountain track of shepherds, gradually widened and improved from age to age… is carried over ground which no engineer, even in alpine countries, would have viewed as practicable." Sited at the top of the pass is the 17th-century Kirkstone Pass Inn – the third highest pub in England.

ST SUNDAY CRAG

St Sunday Crag is a prominent peak in the Patterdale skyline. The peak has a distinctive rounded shape and a long north-east ridge which passes over the tops of Birks and Arnison Crag.

St Sunday is a local name for St Dominic, a Spanish friar who helped found the Dominican order; how this saint's name became attached to the fell is shrouded in mystery. Grisedale Tarn lies below in the lee of the ridge.

ANGLE TARN

A view south-west over Angle Tarn – its spur and two tiny islets clearly visible. Beyond, the land drops away to Brothers Water and the forested fringe of Dovedale. This pretty little tarn is a popular destination for walkers from Patterdale and for more adventurous campers. From this point there are magnificent views in every direction including vistas taking in St Sunday Crag, Nethermost Pike, Helvellyn, Helvellyn Lower Man and the unmistakeable cone-shaped Catstye Cam, Whiteside and Raise.

Although the ascent to the tarn is over 1,000 feet, it is quite an easy walk with few steep sections.

Tarns remain in the bottom of corries when the glacier that formed these wonderful natural amphitheatres fails to cut an exit channel, being forced out and over a lip of harder rock before carrying on its journey down the valley. In warmer times the lip forms a natural dam for water enabling the formation of tarns.

SMALL WATER

Here we see the view north-east from above Harter Fell – the tear-drop shape of Small Water clearly discernible. The Vikings settled in Cumbria in the 10th century. They left a legacy of place names and language in the Lakes. Some key examples include "fell" meaning "hill"; "beck" for "stream"; "tarn" signifying "small lake" and deriving from the Norse for "tear drop"; "holme" meaning "island"; "ghyll" for "ravine"; "howe" for "small hill"; and "thwaite" meaning a "clearing".

BLEA WATER

To the north-west of Small Water lies the larger Blea Water (right), a tarn which is almost as perfect as Small Water itself. Like Small Water it lies beneath the eastern crags of High Street. At 200ft (63m) it is the deepest tarn in the Lake District and is considered to be the finest example of a corrie in England. Its depth was established in 1948 by the Brathay Exploration Group – a key discovery in our understanding of the geology of the British Isles.

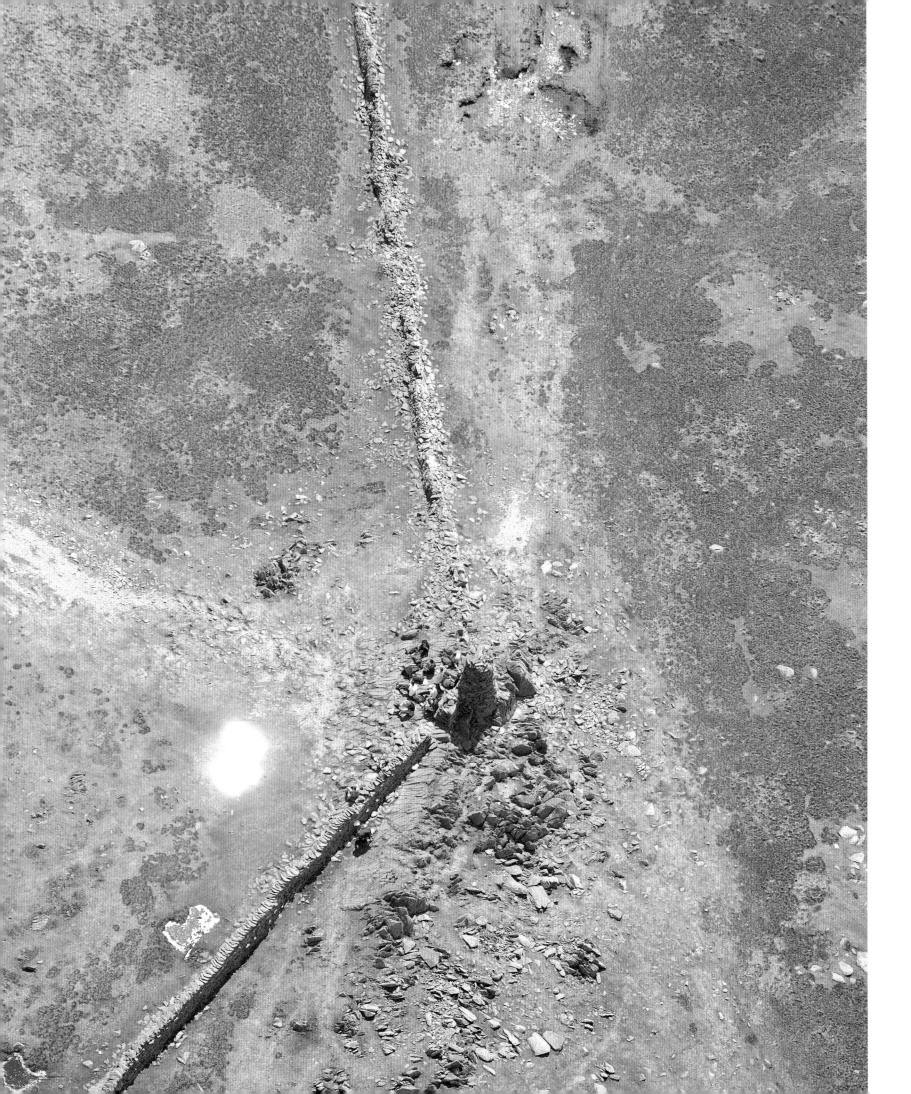

THORNTHWAITE BEACON

To get to Thornthwaite Beacon the best place to start is in the village of Hartsop just off the A592, just before it heads south and up and into the Kirkstone Pass. Heading south out of the village the obvious path runs along Pasture Beck, mounting all the time. At the head of this small valley lies Thornthwaite Cove, with steep cliffs blocking the way ahead apart from a route directly up the southernmost slope. At the top of this the walker attains Thornthwaite Mouth with the Beacon marking the summit of Thornthwaite Crag a few hundred yards further on again to the south. The Beacon is a 14ft (4m) cairn of stones which stands on a natural rock plinth on the highest ground of the fell. The drystone marker indicates a height of 2,572ft (784m).

ILL BELL

The photograph (below) is taken looking over the crags of Ill Bell to the east down into the seemingly opaque waters of the Kentmere Reservoir. This spot is the highest on the uplands between Troutbeck and Kentmere. Ill Bell, together with Yoke and Frostwick, form the western end of the Kentmere Horseshoe. Due south the vista takes in mile upon mile of empty plateau with Buck Crag and the higher ground of Kentmere Park being the main distinctive landmarks. To the south-east the Kentmere Reservoir view opens up to include the Kent river in its own valley snaking away out of the reservoir down to Kentmere village and Burneside where it meets the river Sprint. Beyond lie the southern Lakes.

KENTMERE RESERVOIR

In the early 19th century water-power was king in the valley of the river Kent: there were 90 mills in the upper course of the river alone. The mills took advantage of the raw power of the river – the Kent drops 1,000 feet in 20 miles, and lays claim to be the fastest-flowing river in the country. But the flow was unpredictable and the Kentmere reservoir was constructed in the mid-19th century to even out the water power for the mill-owners. One of the best-preserved mills can be found further down the valley at Barley Bridge in the centre of Staveley. Today, the Kentmere valley is a quiet backwater and it is difficult to believe that 150 years ago there was a working mill for every 315 people living in the valley. The photograph on the right shows the reservoir from high above Thornthwaite Beacon.

NORTHERN LAKE DISTRICT

The Northern Lake District provides some of Britain's most awesome glaciated scenery. It includes everything from volcanic mountains to smooth valley floors – lightly populated and a paradise for the walker after sightings of red deer and other interesting and rare wildlife. Just outside the park proper are many historic villages and towns – all of which deserve more attention than they probably get as the crowds head into the Lakes. This is a landscape that has had a turbulent history – a fact borne out by the many castles that were once pele towers, designed to provide basic protection to local inhabitants when the fierce Border reivers were rampaging. Today, the local pastimes have become more peaceful – embracing everything from walking to windsurfing.

ALLONBY AND MARYPORT

Allonby lies on the Solway Firth estuary in a designated Area of Outstanding Natural Beauty. Today an innocent-enough setting for tourists exploring the shore along the Cumbrian Coastal Way, once the village saw darker dealings as it was on a well-used smugglers' route. From the turn of the 20th century, the long crescent-shaped Allonby Bay has attracted holidaymakers. Among the present-day sights are the hot, cold and vapour baths, built in 1835, now providing elegant private homes.

Maryport is a delightful coastal town on the Solway Firth. It has a history dating back over 2,000 years and visitors today come to a resort that has also been home to a prominent Roman fort, and which boasts elegant Georgian buildings and an extensive set of Victorian docks. Over the centuries the town has been home to many industries including coalmining, iron smelting and shipbuilding. Maryport was formerly known as Ellenfoot but local magnate Humphrey Senhouse changed its name by Deed of Parliament in honour of his wife. The town prospered in Victorian times thanks to the construction of a railway link and its harbour and docks.

ASPATRIA

Aspatria – or "the place of St Patrick's ash tree" – is actually famous for its avenue of yews leading to the site of the first church dedicated to St Kentigern (or Mungo) the first bishop of Glasgow and the saint responsible for bringing Christianity to Cumbria towards the end of the sixth century. The current church was built in 1846-48 and incorporated much of the former structure's stone. There is evidence here of human occupation for over 3,000 years. Aspatria lies at an important junction above the Ellen river valley and on the main route between Maryport and Carlisle. It has been the focus of attack and settlement by Romans, Vikings and Border reivers.

COCKERMOUTH

Cockermouth is an attractive market town just outside the Lake District National Park. It owes its fortunes to the confluence of two rivers – the Cocker and the Derwent. It was the site of a Roman fort and Cockermouth Castle was constructed in the 14th century to defend this strategic spot. Among the most famous names associated with the town are Fletcher Christian, leader of the mutineers on *The Bounty*, the scientist John Dalton and William and Dorothy Wordsworth. Wordsworth clearly loved the town and wrote about it affectionately in his extended biographical poem *The Prelude*:

> *"Retaineth more of ancient homeliness,*
> *Than any other nook of English ground,...*

IREBY (*left and below*)

Today Ireby is a peaceful market town but it was once a bustling place serving the economic needs of the Ellen river valley. Significant evidence of both Bronze Age and Roman settlement has been unearthed in the area. Ireby got its market charter in 1237 and became a thriving corn and sheep market. Important cattle and horse fairs were held here. A sign of the town's affluence is the fact that it could support four inns when the market was at its peak. Ireby church dates back to the 12th century and is one of the town's main attractions. Nearby Overwater Tarn is thought to be haunted by a murdered Jamaican woman – a victim in a real-life tragedy evocative of Bertha Mason in *Jane Eyre*.

GREYSTOKE CASTLE AND VILLAGE

Greystoke is a village on the outskirts of the Lake District National Park. It has retained a village green with, at its centre, an ancient market cross dating back to late Elizabethan times. Around the green are a number of 17th-century houses, a pub and a school founded in 1838. The village church, dedicated to St Andrew, dates back to the mid-1200s although the present structure is Perpendicular in style and owes its existence to the 14th Baron of Greystoke Castle who financed its construction in the late 14th and early 15th centuries. On Church Road is the Sanctuary Stone – symbolically telling of a time when felons could gain sanctuary from pursuers by reaching sanctified ground. A nearby stone is called "Spillers" and is thought to be a plague stone: a place where alms were left to help households in quarantine during an outbreak of the dread disease.

Greystoke Castle was the seat of the Howard family from the 1500s. It started life as a pele tower, was attacked and damaged during the Civil War and burnt down in 1838. The present building was designed in a mock-Elizabethan style by Anthony Salvin. The castle stands in a romantic wooded park. The grounds contain three well-known follies: Bunker's Hill, Fort Putnam, and Spire House. The first two were built to look like fortresses and the last like a church.

LOWTHER CASTLE

Lowther Castle has been the stronghold of the Lowther family for over 900 years. The first recorded structure on the site dates back to the reign of Edward 1. The present building was designed at the height of the Romantic movement in architecture by Robert Smirke, and was built between 1806 and 1814. It was a site of lavish entertainment in the 19th century but could not be maintained in the 20th. Eventually the castle was closed in 1937 and used by a tank regiment during the Second World War; inevitably, a fair bit of damage was caused to nearby drystone walls and bridges. Its contents were removed in the late 1940s and the roof taken away in 1957. There is now a campaign underway to restore the building.

BROUGHAM CASTLE

The Roman fort of Brocavum provided ready-dressed stone for the early Brougham Castle when it was built in the 13th century for the Norman Viewpoint family. By 1268 the castle had passed to Robert Clifford, an important figure in the Scottish wars which started in 1296. He carried out a comprehensive programme of building, significantly improving the castle's defences. The place survived as a residence up until the English Civil War when the building was home to Lady Anne Clifford. She died there in 1676 and soon after the castle was abandoned. It lies two miles outside Penrith and is managed and owned by English Heritage.

PENRITH

Penrith is a large town positioned just outside the Lake District National Park. It was the Cumbrian capital in the 9th and 10th centuries and was included in the Kingdom of Strathclyde. Beacons were lit on Beacon Hill above the town to warn of reiver raids. The castle was built to defend the town and as a sanctuary for the harassed population and was, at one time, owned by Richard Duke of Gloucester, later crowned Richard III. The town has a varied and interesting history. Among one of its most famous attractions is the "giant King of all Cumbria" said to be buried in St Andrew's Churchyard. The spot is marked by four stones that are meant to represent wild boar he killed in nearby Inglewood Forest. It was in Penrith that William and Dorothy Wordsworth and Mary Hutchinson (later to marry William) all attended school.

BRAITHWAITE

Braithwaite (above) is a village of contrasts with a modern northern district, an older heart and an area of more substantial houses to the south. It is found at the foot of the Whinlatter Pass and enjoys spectacular views of Grisedale Pike and Bassenthwaite. It has a reputation as an ideal place from which to explore the northern and central Lakes and has plenty of delightful walking routes on its doorstep. It was this part of the Lakes that was particularly beloved of Alfred Wainwright. His remains were scattered on the top of Haystacks – a nearby fell.

BASSENTHWAITE

The vista south-west across Bassenthwaite with the heights of Bassenthwaite Common and Skiddaw rising out of the valley pastures and woodland. Bassenthwaite is owned by the National Park Authority and at four miles long (6.5km) and ¾ mile (1.2km) wide is one of the largest lakes in the entire region. The lake is also very shallow. There is little settlement around its shores apart from the open-air theatre at Mirehouse – used for a reading in 1974 of *Morte d'Arthur*. Tennyson, who often stayed at Mirehouse, composed much of the poem there. Bassenthwaite is home to the vendace, a rare and endangered fish species found only here and in Derwent Water. It is also an important site for birds including, during the summer months, England's only breeding ospreys.

KESWICK

Today Keswick is an ideal base for exploring the Lakes. Archaeological finds suggest the town's origins go back to Neolithic times. The nearby Castlerigg Stone Circle provides further evidence of this area's importance to our early ancestors. Since 1276 there has been a market in the town of Keswick (from *Cese-wic* – the cheese town), and cheese fairs were held regularly here until the early 20th century.

Medieval Keswick grew up as a ribbon development along either side of the marketplace. By the 19th century small workshops and cottage industries based on wool and leather had developed in the yards adjacent to the houses. Keswick had been a centre for mining activities since Elizabethan times and the discovery of wad (graphite) in a mine in Borrowdale ensured the town became associated with the manufacture of pencils – an industry that survives here to this day. The Moot Hall is probably the most imposing of Keswick's buildings. It dates back to 1571 when it was used as a courthouse. Since then it has been used as a market, prison and town hall.

The town has strong literary associations. William and Dorothy Wordsworth stayed in the town in 1794, Samuel Taylor Coleridge rented part of Greta Hall from 1800-1803, and his brother-in-law, Robert Southey, the Poet Laureate, stayed in Greta Hall for 40 years. It was while living there that he wrote the famous children's story, *The Three Bears*.

SKIDDAW

Two views of Skiddaw looking south-west (above) and north-east (right) – the latter including the northernmost end of Bassenthwaite. Skiddaw is one of the elite group of mountains in England whose summits reach over 3,000 feet. It overlooks Keswick and Derwent Water and is a magnet for walkers. In Victorian times ladies used to ascend the mountain by pony. Skiddaw is the highest fell in this part of the Lake District but its more gradual slopes enable families (including young children) to make the ascent. That said, like all high ground in the Lakes, it is subject to a changeable microclimate and can be exposed to extreme and rapidly changing conditions. In winter the mountain rarely loses its snowcap.

BLENCATHRA

The view of Blencathra (above) looks due north and takes in Middle Tongue with the ridge twisting back on itself to create the higher ground of Sharp Edge. Blencathra lies to the east of Skiddaw. It is one of the Lake District's most famous fells largely because of the popular high walking route along Sharp Edge. It is one of the most northerly mountains in the region and is made up of six separate fell tops, of which the highest is the 2,848ft (868m) Hallsfell Top. There are numerous routes to the top including the one up the arête of Gatesgill or Doddick Fell. More adventurous walkers can tackle the ascent via Scale Tarns and the dramatic Sharp Edge, an exhilarating ridge climb that is as grand as Helvellyn's Striding Edge but without the crowds.

BLENCATHRA

Blencathra used to appear on maps as "the Saddleback" thanks to its shape. It is due to Alfred Wainwright that the older Cumbrian name has enjoyed a revival. The name is thought to be derived from *blaen* (a bare hill top) and *cathrach* (a chair), thus "a bare hill top resembling a chair" – an even more accurate description of the mountain's appearance.

SHARP EDGE

This complex massif boasts two of the Lake District's best ridges: Sharp Edge on the east of the mountain and Halls Fell (Narrow Edge) to the south. Experienced walkers advise a clockwise circuit of the two ridges. The other way is much tougher going with the near-horizontal Sharp Edge making a formidable obstacle to ascend.

Sharp Edge is often described as one of the most challenging walks in the Lakes – not because of steep slopes or boggy ground (both of which can be found) but because of its situation. This poses a real danger to those who attempt it wearing inadequate gear – a problem in the summer when the area's population swells with tourists.

SKELWITH BRIDGE

Skelwith Bridge is situated on the river Brathay near the Wrynose Pass. The village is sited near to a ford across the river; a short distance away is the waterfall called Skelwith Force, which attracts many sightseers. From the 19th century, slate was quarried in the surrounding area and continues today – the material being used for roofing, flooring, paving, lintels and signs. The land that surrounds Skelwith Bridge was described by Wordsworth as a "small and peaceful valley".

CASTLERIGG STONE CIRCLE

Castlerigg Stone Circle is one of the most powerful and spectacular prehistoric monuments in Britain, and is the most visited stone circle in Cumbria. The stone circle is on the level top of a low hill with views across to Skiddaw, Blencathra and Lonscale Fell. There are 38 stones in a circle approximately 100ft (30m) in diameter. Within the ring is a rectangle of a further 10 standing stones. The tallest stone is 7.5ft (2.3m) high. It was probably built around 3000BC – the beginning of the later Neolithic Period – and is one of the earliest stone circles in Britain. It is important in terms of megalithic astronomy and geometry, as the construction contains significant astronomical alignments. Castlerigg Stone Circle was bought in 1913 by a consortium including Canon Hardwick Rawnsley, co-founder of the National Trust.

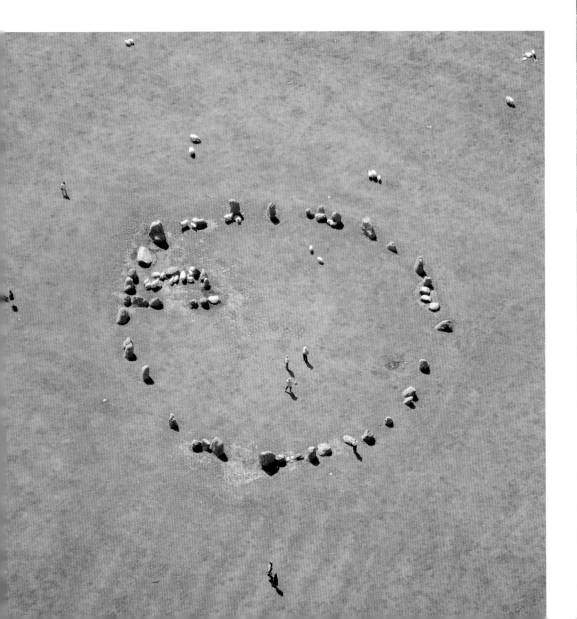

Mosedale And Mosedale Viaduct

Mosedale origin's are Norse and date from 900. Its name comes from the Norse word, *nosi*, for peat moss. Most of the valley to the east of Mosedale contains peat bogs – the remains of a former lake that dried up thousands of years ago. Tiny Mosedale village boasts an early 18th-century Quaker meeting house with fine Tuscan sandstone columns. Nearby, on the summit of volcanic Carrock Fell, are the remains of an oval-shaped Celtic hillfort, the largest in Cumbria. A narrow road leads from the hamlet of Mosedale, follows the river Caldew up the Mosedale valley, and ends at the former Carrock tungsten mine. Lead, copper and small amounts of gold were mined here. The 12-arch Mosedale viaduct (above) is the largest structure along the old Kendal-Penrith railway line. There is an energetic campaign to re-open the link with estimates of between 250,000 and 450,000 passengers a year as potential users of the railway.

POOLEY BRIDGE

Pooley Bridge (left) viewed from over Ullswater looking north-east. The village straddles the river Eamont at the northern end of Ullswater as it flows on to Penrith. The name Pooley Bridge derives from a large pool that used to be found at the mouth of the river Eamont just before it flows out of Ullswater. The bridge dates from the 16th century. Once the village derived its income from fishing and farming and there is still a thriving business serving the needs of anglers who fish for the trout, salmon and the much rarer schelly (a kind of freshwater herring) that live in these waters. The village consists of two main streets lined with delightful old stone houses. One hundred years ago the Ullswater Navigation and Transit Company steamers provided transport for mail, goods and people around Ullswater. Today these same steamers have been converted to carry passengers between Pooley Bridge, Howtown and Glenridding. The village's famous boathouse attracts visitors and photographers from all over the world.

ULLSWATER

Ullswater is the second largest lake in the Lake District. It is serpentine, making three distinct turns, and is 7.5 miles (12km) long; about 3/4 mile (1.2km) wide on average and reaches its greatest depth of 205ft (62m) at Howtown. Ullswater had a dramatic effect on William Wordsworth, and it was beside the Lake that he had an encounter with a field of daffodils that resulted in one of the most famous poems in the language:

> *...I saw a crowd,*
> *A host, of golden daffodils;*
> *Beside the lake, beneath the trees,*
> *Fluttering and dancing in the breeze.*
> *Continuous as the stars that shine*
> *And twinkle on the Milky Way,*
> *They stretch'd in never-ending line*
> *Along the margin of a bay:*
> *Ten thousand saw I at a glance,*
> *Tossing their heads in sprightly dance.*

Many of the Lake District's most famous fell walks start near Ullswater, including the magnificent trek up to Helvellyn's summit via Striding Edge. There are also many less strenuous paths around the lake, rich in spectacle, peace and wildlife. Among the delights are waterfalls such as Aira Force and occasional sightings of wild red deer and red squirrel.

ULLSWATER VIEWS

The calm waters of Ullswater photographed from the north-east looking south-west over Pooley Bridge – the sheltered area around Waterfoot providing an excellent spot to accommodate the large number of moored yachts. The high ground in the distance is Barton Fell with Loadpot Hill in the background.

The name Ullswater is said to derive from "Ulf's water" in memory of Ulf – a Nordic chief who ruled the area. This is yet another proof of the Lake District's deep Viking roots. Even the area's hardy Herdwick sheep (grey wool with white faces) are said to have been introduced by Scandinavian settlers. Before the Vikings, the Romans had a strong presence here. As well as the settlements that line the lake the area also boasts the the world's second largest leadmine in Glenridding (which means "valley of the bracken"). It was on Ullswater that Donald Campbell broke the 200mph world water speed record in 1955. Far less adventurous watersports are the order of the day now and the lake is much used for sailing, sailboarding, fishing and cruising, while the surrounding valleys and mountains provide a vast variety of walks.

GRISEDALE PIKE

Grisedale Pike is the highest summit of the beautiful Coledale Horseshoe. It lies just to the south of the Whinlatter Forest Park. According to some walkers the best ascent is from the village of Braithwaite over the little outlier Kinn and up the east ridge which is quite loose and steep towards the top. The easiest descent is to be made along the north-east ridge which has a broken wall along it and leads down into the Thornthwaite Forest.

HOPEGILL HEAD

This is the view south that greets the visitor with excellent vistas including Hobcarton Crag with Hopegill Head clearly in view to the right of the photograph. These fells are a pleasure to explore in good conditions but can prove very treacherous when it is wet or overcast. The slab-like rocks near the summit of Hopegill Head can become really glassy in wet weather and can prove challenging even for those in modern mountain gear.

HOPEGILL AND HOBCARTON CRAG
A dramatic view of Hopegill Head (the ridge running almost directly towards the front of the photograph) with Hobcarton Crag forming a T-shape on either side. The mountains in the distance include Grasmoor and Crag Hill.